RED RIDING HOOD

There was once a pretty little girl who lived with her mother and father in a cottage near a great wild forest.

One day, a messenger brought her a present from her Grandmother who lived on the other side of the forest.

"I wonder what it can be?" she said as she took some scissors and began to cut through the string. When the parcel was opened there was the most beautiful red cape which, to her delight fitted perfectly. She liked the cape so much that she wore it every day wherever she went. Soon everyone called her Red Riding Hood.

One day, when she was helping her mother to hang out the washing, a letter addressed to Red Riding Hood arrived. She was very excited and asked her mother to read it straight away.

"It is your Grandmother's birthday today," said her mother. "She wants you to have tea with her this afternoon."

Red Riding Hood was pleased. She was very fond of her Grandmother and enjoyed going to her house on the other side of the forest.

Red Riding Hood decided to take her Grandmother some birthday presents. Her mother found her a basket and they packed it with six brown eggs, a pot of honey, some cheese and a large, round fruit cake.

When her father heard about the visit he shook his head and looked very worried. He was one of the King's woodcutters and knew all about the wild forest and its dangers.

"Remember to keep to the long path round the edge of the forest," he told his daughter. "If you try to take a short cut through the trees you might meet the fierce old wolf who lives in the middle of the forest. It isn't safe to go there all by yourself."

After her father's warning Red Riding Hood was very frightened. For a moment she wanted to stay safely at home but then she remembered why she was going on the journey.

"I can't miss Granny's birthday," she thought and, waving goodbye to her parents, she set off on the long road around the forest.

Gradually the sky grew darker and it began to rain. Red Riding Hood felt so wet and cold that her teeth began to chatter. When she came to the top of a hill she could see the roof of her Grandmother's cottage peeping out above the trees.

"If I take the short path through the trees, I'll be there in no time," she thought, and despite her father's warning, she ran down the hill to the edge of the forest.

Red Riding Hood peered into the gloomy
forest. She could see the path twisting ahead
like a pale ribbon among the dark trees. "I'll be
at Granny's much sooner if I hurry through
the forest," she thought and started nervously
along the path. The trees looked very strange,
some of them bent almost double with age,
their branches throwing sinister shadows
across the forest. Red Riding Hood
felt as though hidden eyes were watching her.

She glanced over her shoulder quickly and pulled her cape closer to her.
On she went, deeper into the forest. The path became harder and harder to follow. "Oh dear!" she cried as it twisted first one way and then the other. "I must have taken a wrong turning, the path seems to come to an end at this old tree."

Suddenly Red Riding Hood heard something move in the trees nearby. She spun round and there stood a huge wolf. He had been following her all the time!

Red Riding Hood was very frightened but the wolf bowed deeply and smiled at her.

"Hello, little traveller," he purred. "I see that you have lost your way. Perhaps I can help you? I know the forest rather well."

Astonished at his kindness, Red Riding Hood explained how she was going to have tea with her Grandmother who lived on the other side of the forest.

"The other side of the forest," laughed the wolf, "that's easy: just follow this path through the trees and you'll be there in next to no time!"

Thanking the wolf for his help, Red Riding Hood followed his directions and was soon happily making her way to Granny's cottage.

"That fooled her!" chuckled the wolf
as Red Riding Hood hurried off along the
path which he had shown her. "Now Red
Riding Hood will take hours to reach her
Grandmother's house. If I take the real
road through the forest I'll be there long
before she arrives. There will be plenty of
time to prepare a little surprise..."

The scheming old wolf was right:
when he came to Granny's cottage not a
soul was in sight. He looked all around,
then tiptoed up the garden path and
opened the front door.

When he crept inside, the wolf found the house was empty. He looked in every room but could find no sign of the old lady.

"No matter," he said to himself. "She must have forgotten all about Red Riding Hood and gone out for a walk."

At last Red Riding Hood came to her Grandmother's cottage. She reached up and knocked at the door.

"Come in, child," said a thin, quavering voice from inside the house. "I've been expecting you."

To her surprise, Red Riding Hood found the room in darkness and her Grandmother sitting up in bed with the covers drawn round her.

"It's three o'clock in the afternoon!" she exclaimed.

"Really?" said her Grandmother. "I must have overslept, come closer and let me see you."

"Why Granny, what big eyes you've got," said Red Riding Hood peering through the shadows.

"All the better to see you dear."

"And what big ears you've got," Red Riding Hood continued nervously. She began to feel very uneasy, she wasn't even sure that it was Granny.

"All the better to hear you my dear," smiled Grandmother.

"And such enormous teeth..." gasped Red Riding Hood, stepping back.

"All the better to EAT you!"

At this the wolf sprang out of bed and
snapped his cruel white fangs at Red
Riding Hood.
"I know I'm going to enjoy my
dinner!" he snarled, and chased her
round the room.
"Help!" shrieked the
poor girl, "the wicked wolf
is after me! Oh somebody,
please help!"

No matter where she ran the wolf seemed sure to catch Red Riding Hood. Then, all of a sudden, the door flew open and there stood her father with his trusty crossbow. He took careful aim and killed the wolf with a single shot.

"It's all right," he said as he comforted Red Riding Hood, "the wolf won't harm you now."

"But what about poor Granny?" she sobbed. "The wolf was here when I arrived. How did he get into the house?"

"Don't you worry about her," laughed her father. "Your Grandmother is far too clever to be taken in by a sly old wolf in search of his dinner!"

Red Riding Hood dried her eyes and ran out into the garden. Sure enough, there stood her Grandmother, overjoyed to see her Red Riding Hood safe and sound.

"Oh! I'm so pleased to see you!" she cried. "I was picking some flowers to put on the table when I saw that nasty old wolf come creeping through the trees. I hid behind a bush until he had gone into the house and then I ran to the village to fetch help as quickly as I could. I met your father on the edge of the forest and we hurried back to find you."

"I should have known it wasn't you," laughed Red Riding Hood as she hugged her Grandmother, "his ears were too big!"

Her father came out of the house holding Red Riding
Hood's basket.

"Let's fetch your mother and have our picnic in the
woods," he said.